D0574260

Super Sandcastle: Super Simple DIY (ABDO Publishing) (Libra 12/26/2018

Make a Race Car Your Way!

$18.95

Kids will explore Make a Race Car Your Way! to imagine their own race car. Maybe one that is pushed by a balloon or pulled by a magnet? Then they will use makerspace tools and learn how to get inspired...

#2091349 E. Olson

Grade:123 Dewey:680

Available:12/15/2018 32 pgs

Make a Robo Pet Your Way!

$18.95

Kids will explore Make a Robo Pet Your Way! to imagine their own robo pet. Maybe it wags its tail or its eyes light up? Then they will use makerspace tools and learn how to get inspired, problem-solve,...

#2091350 R. Thomas

Grade:123 Dewey:680

Available:12/15/2018 32 pgs

Make a Spaceship Your Way!

$18.95

Kids will explore Make a Spaceship Your Way! to imagine their own spaceship. Maybe one that flies to Mars or another galaxy? Then they will use makerspace tools and learn how to get inspired, problem-s...

#2091351 R. Thomas

Grade:123 Dewey:680

Available:12/15/2018 32 pgs

SUPER SIMPLE DIY

MAKE A RACE CAR
YOUR WAY!

Elsie Olson

Consulting Editor, Diane Craig,
M.A./Reading Specialist

Super Sandcastle

An Imprint of Abdo Publishing
abdobooks.com

abdobooks.com

Published by Abdo Publishing, a division of ABDO, PO Box 398166, Minneapolis, Minnesota 55439. Copyright © 2019 by Abdo Consulting Group, Inc. International copyrights reserved in all countries. No part of this book may be reproduced in any form without written permission from the publisher. Super SandCastle™ is a trademark and logo of Abdo Publishing.

Printed in the United States of America, North Mankato, Minnesota
102018
012019

THIS BOOK CONTAINS RECYCLED MATERIALS

Design: Sarah DeYoung, Mighty Media, Inc.
Production: Mighty Media, Inc.
Editor: Megan Borgert-Spaniol
Content Consultant: Benjamin J. Garner
Cover Photographs: Shutterstock
Interior Photographs: Archivio Perini ©/Flickr; iStockphoto; Shutterstock

The following manufacturers/names appearing in this book are trademarks: COMP Cams®, Edelbrock®, Fastenal®, Ford® Fusion, Goodyear®, Indianapolis Motor Speedway®, K'NEX® , Mahle®, Mobil®, MOOG®, Nos® Energy Drink, Scotch®, Sunoco®, 3M

Library of Congress Control Number: 2018948783

Publisher's Cataloging-in-Publication Data
Names: Olson, Elsie, author.
Title: Make a race car your way! / by Elsie Olson.
Description: Minneapolis, Minnesota : Abdo Publishing, 2019 | Series: Super simple DIY
Identifiers: ISBN 9781532117183 (lib. bdg.) | ISBN 9781532170041 (ebook)
Subjects: LCSH: Miniature car racing--Juvenile literature. | Handicraft--Juvenile literature. | Creative activities and seat work--Juvenile literature.
Classification: DDC 680--dc23

Super SandCastle™ books are created by a team of professional educators, reading specialists, and content developers around five essential components—phonemic awareness, phonics, vocabulary, text comprehension, and fluency—to assist young readers as they develop reading skills and strategies and increase their general knowledge. All books are written, reviewed, and leveled for guided reading and early reading intervention programs for use in shared, guided, and independent reading and writing activities to support a balanced approach to literacy instruction.

TO ADULT HELPERS

The projects in this book are fun and simple. There are just a few things to remember to keep kids safe. Some projects may use sharp or hot objects. Also, kids may be using messy supplies. Make sure they protect their clothes and work surfaces. Be ready to offer guidance during brainstorming and assist when necessary.

CONTENTS

BECOME A MAKER

A makerspace is like a laboratory. It's a place where ideas are formed and problems are solved. Kids like you create amazing things in makerspaces. Many makerspaces are in schools and libraries. But they can also be in kitchens, bedrooms, and backyards. Anywhere can be a makerspace when you use imagination, inspiration, **collaboration**, and problem-solving!

IMAGINATION

This takes you to new places and lets you experience new things. Anything is possible with imagination!

INSPIRATION

This is the spark that gives you an idea. Inspiration can come from almost anywhere!

MAKERSPACE TOOLBOX

COLLABORATION

Makers work together. They ask questions and get ideas from everyone around them. **Collaboration** solves problems that seem impossible.

PROBLEM-SOLVING

Things often don't go as planned when you're creating. But that's part of the fun! Find creative **solutions** to any problem that comes up. These will make your project even better.

IMAGINE A RACE CAR

DISCOVER AND EXPLORE

Race cars are made to go superfast. Many are built to carry a driver. But some are too small for people. They are driven by **remote** control! You may have seen race cars in books or on TV. Maybe you've even been to an auto race!

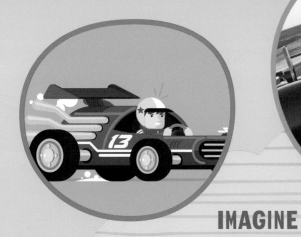

GET INSPIRED!
See page 24

IMAGINE

If you could make any race car, what would it be like? How would it be powered? What features would it have? Would it look like a real-life race car? Or would it be a race car no one has seen before? Remember, there are no rules! Let your imagination run wild!

7

BRING YOUR RACE CAR TO LIFE

It's time to turn your dream race car into a makerspace marvel! What did you like most about your race car? Did it have a **roll cage**? Headlights? Cool stripes? How could you use the materials around you to create these features? Where would you begin?

The Indianapolis Motor Speedway (IMS) in Indiana is home to the Indy 500. This is one of the world's most famous auto races. It's been going on for more than 100 years! The IMS also has a museum. It features many cars that have raced at the speedway.

COLLABORATE!
See page 28

BE SAFE, BE RESPECTFUL

MAKERSPACE ETIQUETTE

THERE ARE JUST A FEW RULES TO FOLLOW WHEN YOU ARE BUILDING YOUR RACE CAR:

1. **ASK FOR PERMISSION AND ASK FOR HELP.** Make sure an adult says it's OK to make your race car. Get help when using sharp tools, such as scissors, or hot tools, like a glue gun.

2. **BE NICE.** Share supplies and space with other makers.

3. **THINK IT THROUGH.** Don't give up when things don't work out exactly right. Instead, think about the problem you are having. What are some ways to solve it?

4. **CLEAN UP.** Put materials away when you are finished working. Find a safe space to store unfinished projects until next time.

GATHER YOUR MATERIALS

Every makerspace has different supplies. Gather the materials that will help you build the race car of your dreams!

STRUCTURE

These are the main materials you will use to build your race car's body.

CONNECTING

These are the materials you will use to hold your race car together.

COLLABORATE!
See page 28

DECORATIONS & DETAILS

These are the materials you will use to make your race car look cool and bring it to life!

⚠ STUCK?

LOOK BEYOND THE USUAL CRAFT SUPPLIES! THE PERFECT SHAPE MIGHT BE IN YOUR KITCHEN CABINET, GARAGE, OR TOY CHEST. SEARCH FOR MATERIALS THAT MIGHT SEEM SURPRISING.

BUILD YOUR RACE CAR'S BODY

Every structure is made up of different shapes. How can you put shapes together to make your dream race car?

INSPIRATION

Most race cars are built to have an **aerodynamic** shape. This means their shape allows for quick and easy movement through air. What other objects are aerodynamic?

GET INSPIRED!
See page 24

⚠ STUCK?

TIRES, HUBCAPS, AND STEERING WHEELS ARE ROUND. LOOK FOR EVERYDAY ITEMS, LIKE PLATES, COINS, AND BOTTLE CAPS, THAT HAVE A SIMILAR SHAPE.

HOW WILL YOUR RACE CAR GO?

What will power your race car? Knowing this will help you figure out what materials you could use to construct your race car.

Will it be powered by your feet?

Then you need a structure that fits around your body. You will also need a way to connect it to your body!

PROBLEM-SOLVE!
See page 26

Will it be
powered by
balloons?

Then you will need
a way to easily blow
up the balloons.

IMAGINE

WHAT IF YOUR RACE CAR NEEDED TO FLY OR FLOAT?
HOW WOULD THAT CHANGE YOUR RACE CAR?

Italian **designer** Giorgetto Giugiaro is one of the most famous car designers of the last 100 years. He has designed race cars, luxury cars, and everyday **vehicles**. His company has designed more than 200 cars!

Will it be pulled by a magnet? Then you need to attach magnetic materials to the car.

magnet

16

COLLABORATE!
See page 28

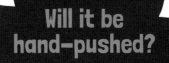

Will it be hand-pushed? Then you need wheels that turn easily.

⚠ STUCK?

YOU CAN ALWAYS CHANGE YOUR MIND IN A MAKERSPACE. IS YOUR MAGNET-POWERED CAR NOT WORKING RIGHT? YOU CAN TURN IT INTO A HAND-PUSHED CAR INSTEAD!

Some wheels have narrow cuts called treads on their surface for gripping the road.

17

CONNECT YOUR RACE CAR

Will your race car be **permanent**? Or will you take it apart when you are finished? Knowing this will help you decide what materials to use.

TOTALLY **TEMPORARY**

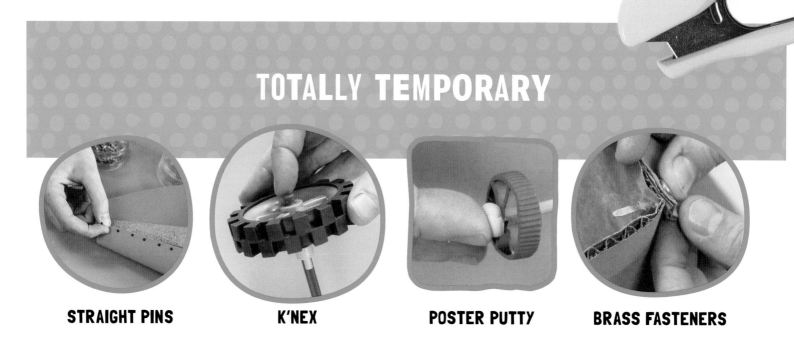

STRAIGHT PINS **K'NEX** **POSTER PUTTY** **BRASS FASTENERS**

PROBLEM-SOLVE!
See page 26

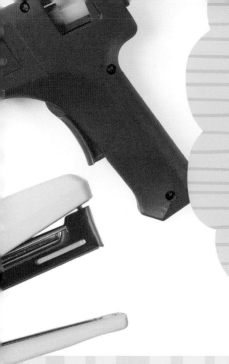

IMAGINE

WHAT IF YOUR RACE CAR WERE MADE OF SNACKS YOU CAN EAT? OR IF IT WERE MADE ONLY WITH ITEMS IN YOUR RECYCLING BIN? WHAT MATERIALS WOULD YOU USE TO CONNECT IT?

A LITTLE STICKY

SUPER STICKY

CLEAR TAPE

STAPLES

ELECTRICAL TAPE

DUCT TAPE

DECORATE YOUR RACE CAR

TISSUE PAPER

Decorating is the final step in making your race car. It's where you add **details** to your car. How do your decorations bring your race car to life?

PUSHPINS AND GEMS

GET INSPIRED!
See page 24

WRAPPING PAPER TUBES AND FOIL TAPE

PAPER CLIPS AND STRAW

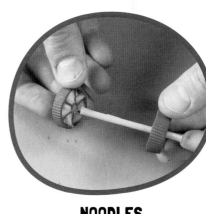

PAPER PLATES WITH METAL CONTAINERS

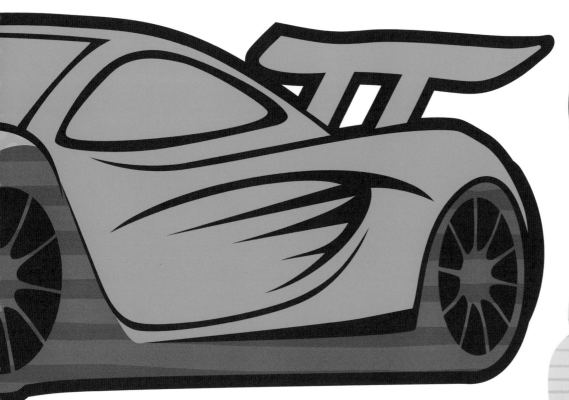

NOODLES

IMAGINE

WHO WILL DRIVE YOUR RACE CAR?

21

HELPFUL HACKS

As you work, you might discover ways to make challenging tasks easier. Try these simple tricks and **techniques** as you construct your race car!

Use mounting tape to attach materials that may need to be reused, such as magnets.

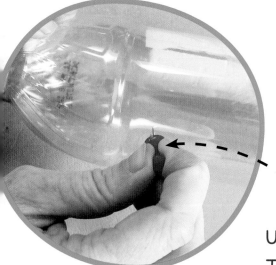

Use a pushpin to poke a hole. Then use a sharpened pencil to make the hole wider.

PROBLEM—SOLVE!
See page 26

Use hook-and-loop tape to make a hood that can open and close.

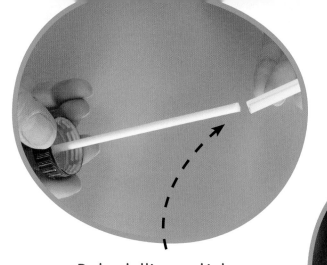

Bend paper clips into the shape you want with a needle-nose pliers.

Put a lollipop stick inside a straw for an **axle** that turns easily. Attach wheels to the lollipop stick.

⚠ STUCK?

MAKERS AROUND THE WORLD SHARE THEIR PROJECTS ON THE INTERNET AND IN BOOKS. IF YOU HAVE A MAKERSPACE PROBLEM, THERE'S A GOOD CHANCE SOMEONE ELSE HAS ALREADY FOUND A SOLUTION. SEARCH THE INTERNET OR LIBRARY FOR HELPFUL ADVICE AS YOU MAKE YOUR PROJECTS!

GET INSPIRED

Get inspiration from the real world before you start building your race car!

LOOK AT RACE CARS

Look up pictures of real-life race cars. They may have **roll cages** or **spoilers**. What other features do you notice? How can you combine these features in your race car?

LOOK AT A PARKING LOT

Race cars have many of the same features as everyday cars, trucks, and buses. Walk around a parking lot or watch **vehicles** drive along the street. What do you notice about them? How could they inspire your race car?

LOOK AT OTHER VEHICLES

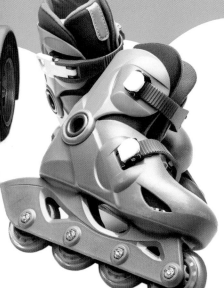

Like race cars, airplanes are **designed** to be **aerodynamic**. Bicycles and roller skates have wheels. Boats have steering wheels. Let these vehicles inspire you as you design your race car!

PROBLEM-SOLVE

No makerspace project goes exactly as planned. But with a little creativity, you can find a **solution** to any problem.

FIGURE OUT THE PROBLEM

Maybe your balloon car isn't moving. Why do you think this is happening? Thinking about what may be causing the problem can lead you to a solution!

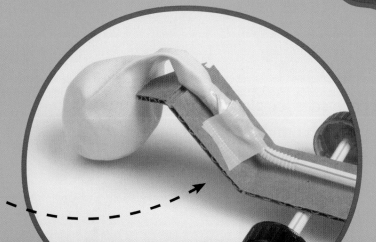

★
SOLUTION:
Build a lighter body out of cardboard.

★
SOLUTION:
Add a second balloon for more power.

BRAINSTORM AND TEST

Try coming up with three possible **solutions** to any problem.
Maybe your wheels aren't turning easily. You could:

1. Add rubber band tires so the wheels grip the surface better.

2. Test the wheels on a different surface, such as carpet instead of a smooth table.

3. Try different materials for the wheels, **axles**, or both.

Test all three and see which works best!

ADAPT

Still stuck? Try a different material or change the **technique** slightly.

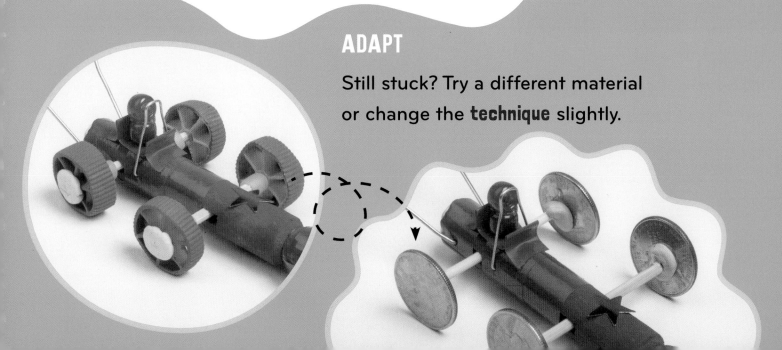

COLLABORATE

Collaboration means working together with others. There are tons of ways to collaborate to build a race car!

ASK A FELLOW MAKER

Talk to a friend, classmate, or family member. Other makers can help you think through the different steps to building a race car. These helpers can also lend a pair of hands during construction!

ASK AN ADULT HELPER

This could be a teacher, librarian, grandparent, or any trusted adult. Describe what you want a material to do instead of asking for a specific material. Your helper might think of items you didn't know existed!

ASK AN EXPERT

A car repair person or other **expert** could explain how the parts of a car work together. A car salesperson can talk about different types of cars and their features. An automobile engineer could tell you about new kinds of cars being invented!

29

THE WORLD IS A MAKERSPACE!

Your race car may look finished, but don't close your makerspace toolbox yet. Think about what would make your race car better. What would you do differently if you built it again? What would happen if you used different **techniques** or materials?

IMAGINATION

INSPIRATION

COLLABORATION

PROBLEM-SOLVING

DON'T STOP AT RACE CARS

You can use your makerspace toolbox beyond the makerspace! You might use it to accomplish everyday tasks, such as school papers or yard work. But makers use the same toolbox to do big things. One day, these tools could help build roadways or explore outer space. Turn your world into a makerspace! What problems could you solve?

GLOSSARY

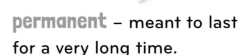

aerodynamic – having qualities that allow for easy and quick movement through air.

axle – a bar that connects two wheels.

collaborate – to work with others.

designer – someone who creates a sketch or outline of something that will be made. To design is to plan how something will appear or work.

detail – a small part of something.

expert – a person who is very knowledgeable about a certain subject.

hubcap – the cap over the center of a wheel.

permanent – meant to last for a very long time.

remote – acting from a distance.

roll cage – a strong frame that helps protect the driver of a car if the car crashes.

solution – an answer to, or a way to solve, a problem.

spoiler – a narrow plate that prevents an automobile from lifting off the ground at high speeds.

technique – a method or style in which something is done.

vehicle – a machine used to carry people or goods.